DATE DUE

MAR 0 6 2011	MAR 2 5 2013
JUN 15 2011	APR 0 2 2013
JUL 19 2011	JUN 12 2013
OCT 10 2011	AUG 0 7 2013
DEC 03 2011	MAR 18 2014
APR 19 2012	MAR 03 2018
MAY 29 2012	APR 16 2018
JUL 03 2012	
JUL 20 2012	
AUG 09 2012	
AUG 28 2012	
SEP 12 2012	
OCT 11 2012	
NOV 05 2012	
DEC 05 2012	
JAN 24 2013	
FEB 19 2013	

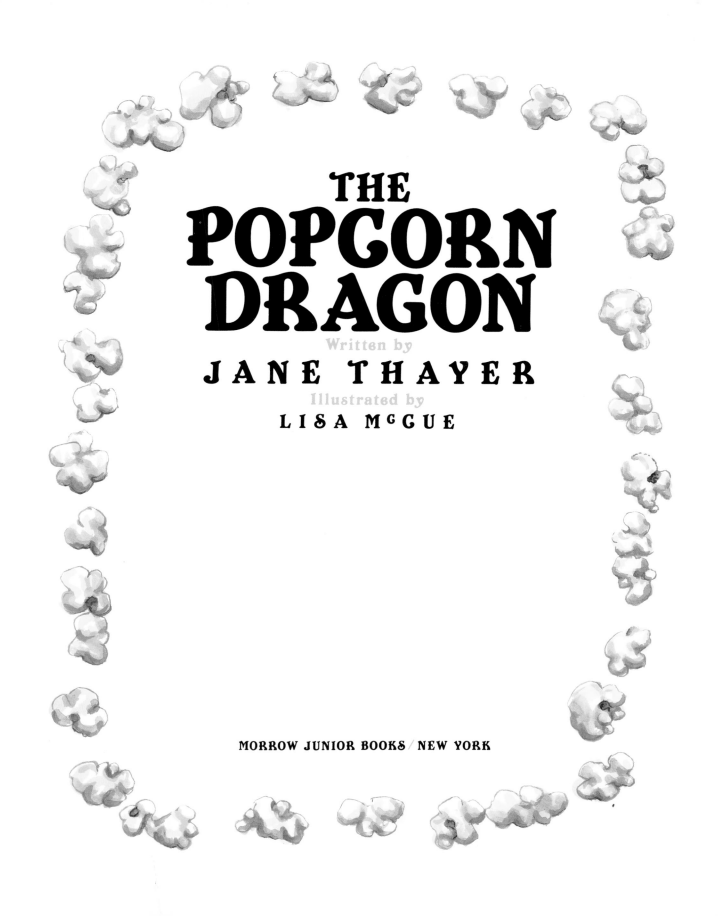

THE
POPCORN
DRAGON

Written by

JANE THAYER

Illustrated by

LISA McCUE

MORROW JUNIOR BOOKS / NEW YORK

To the Cooks, who knew Dexter first

Printed in Singapore.
10
Library of Congress Cataloging-in-Publication Data
Thayer, Jane.
The popcorn dragon / by Jane Thayer; illustrations by Lisa McCue.
p. cm.
Summary: Though his hot breath is the envy of all the other
animals, a young dragon learns that showing off does not make
friends.
ISBN 0-688-08340-4. ISBN 0-688-08876-7 (lib. bdg.)
[1. Dragons—Fiction.] I. McCue, Lisa, ill. II. Title.
PZ7.W882Po 1989
[E]—dc19   88-39855   CIP   AC

Dexter was a dragon with a green scaly body and a long twisty tail. He had short knobby legs. He had wings like a bat's, which he would be able to fly with when he was older.

Like all dragons, Dexter had a hot breath. When he got mad or excited and breathed extra hard, his breath grew extra hot.

One day Dexter felt sad because he had no one to play with. He was so sad that he sighed a deep sigh. Out of his mouth came a cloud of smoke! "Why, look at me!" said Dexter. "I'm blowing smoke!"

He could hardly believe it. He sat still and breathed hard. Sure enough, smoke was coming out of his mouth. Dexter cried, "I never knew I could blow smoke!"

He ran to his mother, panting for joy. He shouted, "Look at me blowing smoke!"

He ran to the edge of the river where he could see
himself in the water. He said, "Just look at that smoke!"
He thought, I'm going to show the other animals how I
can blow smoke!

Dexter began to stroll up and down. He puffed a little smoke here. He puffed a little smoke there, as if blowing smoke was just nothing. After a while he saw the other animals — the giraffe, the zebra, and the elephant — peeking at him from behind some rocks.

The giraffe, the zebra, and the elephant all came out
and watched Dexter blowing smoke.

Their eyes nearly popped out of their heads. Dexter
blew smoke till he looked like a bonfire.

Pretty soon the giraffe slipped quietly away and hid behind a rock. He said, "Whoof," trying to blow smoke like Dexter. But he couldn't do it.

Then the zebra ran off and disappeared over a hill. He
said, "Whh," and "Whh," trying to blow smoke like
Dexter. But he couldn't do it.

Finally the elephant said, "Good-by, I have to go." He
trotted into the woods and went, "Whoo, whoo, whoo,"
trying to blow smoke like Dexter. But he couldn't. So he
said, "Pooh! Who wants to blow smoke!"

They all came back and watched Dexter out of the corner of their eyes to see how he blew smoke.

Dexter was delighted. He said, "I can blow smoke and you can't!" Dexter pranced around, showing off. He chased a yellow butterfly with his smoke. He puffed a cloud of smoke at a green grasshopper. He scared a striped chipmunk with his smoke.

He even puffed a small puff, accidentally, of course, right at the other animals. The smoke felt rather warm to the other animals. The giraffe said, "You stop it!" The zebra said, "*I'm* going home!"

Dexter stopped blowing smoke. He thought, I don't want them to go home. He said loudly, "Oh, I guess I won't blow plain smoke any more. I think I will blow smoke *rings!*" He stuck his head straight up in the air and blew smoke rings.

The other animals just had to watch Dexter blow smoke rings. They moved back a little, so they wouldn't get scorched. They watched till they were so envious they could hardly stand it.

Finally the elephant said, "Certainly is silly, blowing smoke rings." He started to stalk away.

Dexter stopped blowing smoke rings. He thought, What can I do to make them stay? He said loudly, "Oh, I guess I won't blow plain smoke rings any more. I think I will blow smoke rings around my *tail!*"

He turned his head and blew smoke rings around his tail. He switched his tail this way and blew rings around it. He switched his tail that way and blew rings around it. Finally he switched so hard he hit himself in the nose. The blow brought tears to his eyes. Dexter blinked quickly and said, "See? I can even hit myself in the nose!"

The animals were so envious, not knowing how
Dexter's nose hurt, that they couldn't bear to watch one
more minute.

The zebra said, "That Dexter is always showing off!"
The giraffe said, "We don't like him, do we!"
The elephant said, "Come on. Let's go!"

When Dexter saw the other animals actually going, he stopped blowing smoke rings. Suddenly he remembered that he wanted someone to play with. He called out hopefully, "Want me to come with you?"

The giraffe said no, they didn't.

Dexter watched them go. Then he went home and said to his mother in a forlorn voice, "I haven't got anything to do."

His mother said, "Blow some smoke." "I don't feel like it," said Dexter. His mother said, "Go play with the other animals." "They won't play with me," said Dexter. "Then you must have been showing off," his mother said.

Dexter wandered down the road to where the other animals were playing. He did wish he could play too. He sat down to watch.

The zebra shouted, "We don't like you. Go away!"

Dexter was very sorry now that he had showed off. He had no one to play with. He was tired of blowing smoke. He wandered into a cornfield and lay down in the shade of the tall cornstalks.

He watched a yellow butterfly flutter against the blue sky. He watched a green grasshopper hop on a blade of green grass. The butterfly and grasshopper did not know or care how lonely Dexter felt. He could hear the far-off voices of the animals playing.

The sun was warm. The sound of insects and the far-off voices began to make Dexter drowsy. His eyes closed. He fell asleep.

Dexter began to dream fireworks were going off. Then he dreamed the most delicious smell in the world. He woke up. He heard, *Pop, pop, pop!*

"*Popcorn!*" cried Dexter.

Right under his nose was an ear of corn that had fallen off the stalk onto the ground.

Dexter's hot breath was popping the corn on the ear. *Pop, pop, pop,* the kernels came popping out.

Dexter reached out and gobbled some. *Crunch, crunch, smack, gobble, gulp.* "Mmm! Good!" said Dexter.

Soon the popcorn on the ground was all gone. Dexter wanted some more. He stood on his hind legs and pulled the husks off an ear of corn on a cornstalk. Then, very carefully, Dexter breathed his hot breath on the ear of corn. *Pop* went the corn. *Pop, pop, pop, pop!* The crisp white kernels fell in a shower.

The popcorn smell began to drift through the air. The giraffe, the zebra, and the elephant stopped their playing. They said, "Mmm! Popcorn!"

They put their noses up in the air and went *sniff, sniff* toward the smell.

When Dexter looked up from his crunching, they were peeking around the cornstalks. Dexter swallowed the popcorn. He said quickly, "Have some?"

The giraffe, the zebra, and the elephant cried, "But you've eaten it all up!"

Dexter said, "I'll pop more!"

He moved eagerly along the row of cornstalks to a new place and quickly pulled off some of the husks. His hot breath started to pop the corn. The popcorn fell all around. The animals crunched and munched. Soon the popcorn was gone.

Dexter said quickly, for fear they would go away, "I'll pop some more if you want."

The animals looked at each other. The giraffe said, "That Dexter is very nice when he doesn't show off."

The zebra said, "Let's ask him to play with us."

The elephant said to Dexter, "Want to play with us, Dexter?"

Dexter cried, "O.K.!"

He was so delighted that before he knew it he breathed a little hard—and out came a cloud of smoke! But Dexter quickly turned his head to one side.

"Oh, excuse me, please!" he said politely.

And when they had played until they were hungry,
Dexter popped popcorn for everyone.